D0547062

Biography of The World's Richest Woman

The Life And Legacy Of Francoise Bettencourt Meyers

Blake Hayden

Copyright © 2023 Blake Hayden. All rights reserved. No part of this book may be reproduced, stored in a retrieval system, or transmitted in any form or by any means, electronic, mechanical, photocopying, recording, or otherwise, without prior written permission from the copyright owner.

Table Of Contents

Introduction

Few names are as revered in the halls of power and riches as the Bettencourt clan.

Their story is one of ageless beauty, extraordinary commercial prowess, and a lasting impact on the cosmetics industry.

Francoise Bettencourt Meyers, the heir to one of the biggest and most prosperous cosmetics empires, L'Oreal, is at the center of this incredible narrative.

The roots of the Bettencourt tradition may be discovered in the brilliant businessman Eugene Schueller, who established L'Oreal at the turn of the 20th century.

.

In this biography, we set out on a quest to learn more about the extraordinary Francoise Bettencourt Meyers, who was charged with guarding this mighty treasure.

From her early years to her present role as chairperson of L'Oreal, Francoise has had the opportunity of living a life that is also quite responsible.

However, this story is more than simply one of wealth and success; it also examines a woman's quest to rise beyond her family's wealth and accept a greater calling.

We will learn about her unrelenting devotion to social problems, her constant quest for knowledge, and her determination to leave a lasting impression on the world as we learn more about her life.

Chapter 1

Passing on a Legacy

The name Bettencourt reverberates throughout the annals of industrial achievement as a monument to tenacity, creativity, and the limitless potential of desire.

The history of the Bettencourt family can be traced back to Eugene Schueller, a brilliant scientist, and businessman who developed L'Oreal, a legendary beauty brand that would permanently change the world's cosmetics sector.

It took pure tenacity for Eugene Schueller to make the bold transition from a little laboratory to establishing a massive empire in the cosmetics industry.

Schueller set out on a quest to redefine beauty standards and boost the self-esteem of millions of people throughout the globe, armed with a love for chemistry and an unwavering faith in the transformational potential of beauty products.

Francoise's Upbringing and Family Background.

Francoise Bettencourt Meyers, who was born into this distinguished family, acquired more than just riches and status; she was raised in a world of luxury and enormous responsibility.

The L'Oreal enterprise was supported by her parents, Liliane Bettencourt and Andre Bettencourt, who gave it unshakable devotion.

Francoise was raised with qualities of humility, kindness, and a strong work ethic despite the luxury around her.

The value of utilizing money as a vehicle for good change was ingrained in her by her parents; this idea would have a big impact on her future undertakings.

Influence of Her Grandfather, Eugene Schueller, on Her Life

Eugene Schueller, Francoise's grandpa, had an even greater impact on her life than his riches and status.

The L'Oreal founder's pioneering attitude permeated subsequent generations, profoundly influencing Francoise's outlook and goals.

Francoise used to listen in wonder to stories about her grandfather's never-ending quest for invention, his ground-breaking studies, and his steadfast dedication to providing the best beauty products to women all over the globe.

Francoise was impressed by Eugene Schueller's innovative business strategy and his love of science, which sowed the seeds of a lifetime obsession with the cosmetics industry.

Moreover, Francoise's goals were guided by Eugene Schueller's dedication to charity and social responsibility.

He believed that companies had a responsibility to give back to society, a belief that Francoise would uphold throughout her adult life.

As she became older, Francoise realized that she carried a heavy burden and that it was up to her to uphold her family's reputation of greatness and generosity.

The pressure of expectations didn't scare her; instead, it drove her determination to forge her path and add her mark to the illustrious history of the Bettencourt family.

Chapter 2

The Empowered Heiress

As Francoise Bettencourt Meyers reached adulthood, she found herself on the verge of a brand-new era—a period of change and responsibility.

She was the only inheritor of the storied L'Oreal Corporation after the death of her grandmother, Liliane Bettencourt.

Being in the limelight required more than simply inheriting significant wealth; it also required taking on the role of leader for a worldwide brand that had come to stand for empowerment, innovation, and beauty.

She carried the heritage of L'Oreal on her shoulders. Francoise, though, accepted her new position with poise and a sense of mission.

She realized that providing goods that empowered women, boosted their confidence, and recognized their uniqueness was the key to her family's success, which went beyond money and profits.

Navigating the Complexities of Family Business and Corporate Leadership

It was not easy to run a family company of this size. Francoise had to deal with the complicated web of shareholder expectations, business governance, and familial relationships.

She nonetheless overcame these difficulties with grace and a determination to advance the business.

Francoise understood the need of maintaining the traditions and ideals that had made L'Oreal successful for decades while also embracing innovation to stay up with the fast-changing beauty business.

Executives, researchers, and staff at L'Oreal were encouraged to collaborate and be creative by her inclusive leadership style.

Francoise also accepted the duty of managing the organization's abundant resources and guiding them toward endeavors that mirrored her basic values of sustainability, diversity, and social impact.

She aimed to increase L'Oreal's dedication to moral corporate conduct so that it might continue to have a positive influence on the globe.

Her Early Ventures into the World of Business and Philanthropy.

Francoise set out on a personal adventure of discovery and generosity beyond the confines of L'Oreal.

She was aware that her goals went beyond the boardroom, and she was determined to utilize her clout to bring about change.

Francoise founded the Bettencourt Schueller Foundation to fund scholarly endeavors, artistic endeavors, and charitable endeavors, drawing motivation from her grandfather's generous history. She promoted the arts, historical preservation, and the promotion of medical advances via the foundation, demonstrating the blending of corporate savvy with humanitarian vision.

Francoise's charitable endeavors also included causes near her heart, such as environmental protection and gender equality.

Beyond just sending checks, she actively participated in the initiatives and causes she backed, utilizing her money and voice to promote a more just and equal society.

Chapter 3

Social Impact and Philanthropy

Francoise Bettencourt Meyers discovered her true calling outside of the glitz of the business world in the field of charity.

She committed herself to social issues that reflected her basic principles because she felt a strong sense of duty and a sincere desire to improve the lives of others.

Her charitable initiatives were motivated by compassion for the underprivileged and a dedication to advancing social justice. Francoise aggressively sought out initiatives and programs that addressed critical social challenges, such as healthcare access, cultural preservation, and poverty reduction.

She stands out as a philanthropist with a genuine enthusiasm for making a difference because of her personal commitment and hands-on approach.

She acknowledged the luxury of her upbringing and utilized her riches to actively interact with the areas and people she wished to assist, rather than merely writing checks.

The Creation and Expansion of the Bettencourt Schueller Foundation

The founding and growth of the Bettencourt Schueller Foundation played a key role in Francoise's charitable legacy.

The foundation, which bears her grandpa Eugene Schueller's name and honors her family's history, has grown to be a potent tool for generating good social effects.

The foundation's mission was greatly broadened under Francoise's direction.

It catalyzed ground-breaking studies in many sectors, advancing research, initiatives for cultural preservation, and international humanitarian endeavors.

Francoise believed that the arts, culture, and tradition played a crucial part in enhancing lives and developing a more compassionate world, and the foundation was dedicated to preserving these aspects of society.

Efforts Towards Environmental Sustainability and Women Empowerment

Francoise became an outspoken supporter of sustainability and environmental conservation after seeing the pressing need to solve environmental issues.

She sponsored programs via her foundation and her initiatives that promoted eco-friendly activities and looked for cutting-edge ways to address climate change.

Additionally, Francoise utilized her position to empower women and advance gender equality since she was a fervent supporter of women's rights. She understood that a fair and equitable society needed to have gender parity.

To help women overcome socioeconomic obstacles and realize their full potential, she backed initiatives that offered them access to education and vocational training.

Francoise increased the reach of her charitable work and encouraged others to join her in the quest for a more just and sustainable society via her commitment to environmental sustainability and women's empowerment.

Chapter 4

Transformational Leadership

Francoise Bettencourt Meyers stepped into the shoes of a history that spanned decades when she became the chairperson of L'Oreal.

Despite carrying the weight of the greatest cosmetics firm in the world, Francoise led with composure and confidence that inspired everyone around her.

She accepted the obligation of serving as a role model for women who want to hold leadership positions and understood the importance of her position as a female leader in a field that is mostly male.

Her ascension to the top of L'Oreal was driven by a strong sense of purpose and a vision for the future of the firm, not merely by inheriting the position.

Innovations and Strategies that Drove L'Oreal's Continued Success

L'Oreal continues to thrive as a leading force in the global beauty industry under Francoise's shrewd guidance.

She was aware that the cosmetics market was always changing due to altering customer needs and fashion trends. She was the driving force behind the company's innovation and research culture to remain ahead in this fast-paced environment.

To explore novel formulas and cutting-edge technology, Francoise urged L'Oreal's scientists and researchers to push the envelope.

Due to its dedication to research and development, the firm has constantly produced ground-breaking goods that satisfy a wide range of customer demands.

She also embraced digital change, seeing the potential of social media and e-commerce to reshape the beauty sector.

L'Oreal was able to develop long-lasting brand loyalty because of its strategic investments in digital marketing and individualized online experiences.

Balancing Personal Life with Responsibilities as a Business Leader

Francoise struggled to strike a balance between the demands of her personal life and her obligations as a corporate leader and an empowered heiress.

She managed the complexities of her several roles—she was not only the chairperson but also a wife and a mother, with composure and grace.

Francoise recognized the need of striking a balance between job and family obligations.

Despite her busy schedule, she made an effort to prioritize spending time with her loved ones, making sure that her children knew she was there for them.

Francoise was motivated by her family's heritage and understood the importance of raising the next generation.

As her parents and grandparents had done for her, she supported her children's achievements and encouraged them to follow their ambitions.

Chapter 5

Challenges and Controversies

Francoise Bettencourt Meyers had her fair share of difficulties as a result of her public life.

She found herself in the heart of disputes that captured the interest of the public and the media because she was the heiress to a sizable wealth and a well-known businessperson. The legal dispute about her inheritance was one of the biggest issues. Due to the intricacy of her family's riches, several parties who wanted a piece of the Bettencourt estate filed lawsuits and conflicts.

The legal team representing Francoise had to negotiate complex financial arrangements and justify her legitimate claim to the family's assets.

In addition, her private life came under investigation since tabloids and photographers wanted to know everything about her relationships and extramarital encounters. Francoise wanted to keep her family and friends out of the spotlight, but because of her fame, she found it difficult to do so.

Media scrutiny and legal disputes over the Bettencourt family

Over the years, the riches and power of the Bettencourt family drew media attention, and this attention wasn't always positive.

Investigations and legal actions were prompted by claims of financial irregularity and dubious business activities against the family.

These court cases placed the Bettencourt family in the spotlight, damaging their image and suffering them considerable pain. Francoise, who was in charge of running the family's commercial empire, had to bear the brunt of these difficulties in particular.

How She Survived Adversity and Kept Her Cool and Dignity

Francoise Bettencourt Meyers showed extraordinary fortitude and poise throughout the storms of disputes and difficulties.

She stayed firm in her devotion to her family's tradition and to the principles she held dear despite the personal and professional difficulties.

Her persistent commitment to her values and unflinching faith in the power of integrity allowed her to preserve her dignity in the face of hardship.

Francoise confronted the issues head-on, working with the authorities and upholding openness to resolve any issues that were brought up.

Additionally, she found comfort in her charitable work, utilizing her money and position to improve society.   She was able to find meaning outside of the spotlight of the media and the court fights by immersing herself in causes that meant a great deal to her.

Francoise also relied on the support of her loved ones through the trying times. Her close-knit family and friends served as a source of support and inspiration, serving as a constant reminder of the principles that guided her path.

Chapter 6

Motherhood, Love, and Family

Francoise Bettencourt Meyers discovered love and friendship in the arms of Jean-Pierre Meyers away from the sparkle and glamour of the corporate world.

Their marriage, which brought together the Meyers and Bettencourt families, two powerful families, solidified their relationship on a personal and professional level.

Being a successful businessman in his own right, Jean-Pierre contributed a lot of knowledge and understanding to the partnership.

Their close relationship was built on a foundation of similar principles and mutual respect, which allowed them to understand and support one another while they dealt with the challenges of their high-profile existence.

Francoise and Jean-Pierre demonstrated the strength of cooperation and togetherness as a marriage, utilizing their combined influence to promote improvement in both business and charity.

Her Role as a Mother and the Passing of the Baton to the Next Generation

Francoise used the same passion and commitment she showed in her professional life to her job as a loving mother.

She made it a point to be there and actively engaged in her children's lives despite the pressures of her leadership role at L'Oreal and her charitable endeavors.

Francoise fostered a nurturing and caring atmosphere for her kids, encouraging them to follow their dreams and discover their hobbies.

She saw the necessity of teaching the next generation the virtues of perseverance, honesty, and social responsibility so they might become leaders in their way.

Francoise got ready to hand the reins of power to the Meyers family of Bettencourt to the next generation as time went on.

To ensure a seamless transfer and the continuation of the family heritage, she prepared her children to assume significant positions within the family company and foundation.

Reflections on the Past of Her Family and Future Goals

Francoise found inspiration and direction from following in the footsteps of her ancestors as she thought back on the illustrious history of the Bettencourt family.

She recognized the value of tenacity, invention, and generosity in determining her family's success and was grateful for the teachings received from her parents, Liliane and Andre Bettencourt, as well as her grandpa, Eugene Schueller.

Her goals for the future went well beyond professional success. Francoise wanted to leave a lasting legacy of kindness, contribution to society, and sustainability.

She aimed to create a legacy for her family that would endure and leave a good mark on the world.

Francoise used her memories of her family's past as a compass to help her make choices that were consistent with her goals for the future.

She understood that her family had a special chance and obligation to create a better world for future generations because of the power and influence they had.

Chapter 7

Maintaining a Viable Legacy

As Francoise Bettencourt Meyers established herself as L'Oreal's chairperson, she recognized the need of preserving the organization's history while guiding it toward a future of sustained prosperity and innovation.

Francoise Bettencourt took on the challenge of running one of the most recognizable beauty companies in the world by building on the foundation her grandpa Eugene Schueller created and fostered by her parents Liliane and Andre Bettencourt.

L'Oreal kept making investments in cutting-edge technology and pushed the boundaries of skincare, haircare, and cosmetics under her direction.

The organization's commitment to ethical sourcing and sustainable business practices further solidified its position as a market leader.

Francoise encouraged bravery and originality among the teams at L'Oreal by fostering an innovative culture inside the organization.

L'Oreal was able to stay relevant and durable in the face of evolving market trends because of her ability to find a balance between upholding the brand's tradition and embracing modernity.

The Bettencourt Meyers Family's Business Goals for the Future

The Bettencourt Meyers family had goals for the future beyond L'Oreal and business success. Their goal was to establish socially conscious, environmentally friendly enterprises that would benefit society.

The family aimed to increase the Bettencourt Schueller Foundation's impact and scope out of a common philanthropic commitment.

They sought to use their money to significantly improve people's lives by supporting more artistic endeavors, educational programs, and humanitarian causes.

The family's objective included encouraging business and developing new skills.

They wanted to make it possible for ambitious company owners, especially women, to pursue their entrepreneurial dreams and have a positive impact on the world economy.

Her Long-Lasting Effects on Society and the Beauty Industry

Beyond her position as a commercial leader, Francoise Bettencourt Meyers had a significant impact on the social landscape and the beauty industry. Her dedication to ethical behavior, social responsibility, and environmental sustainability established standards for other beauty companies to meet.

Her support for women's rights and gender equality struck a chord with people all across the globe, empowering a new generation of female leaders to break down barriers and take up their proper positions in the business world.

Furthermore, Francoise's commitment to charity and her family's history of altruism served as an example of how money can change lives when it is handled sensibly and with compassion.

Her efforts not only made numerous people's lives better, but they also demonstrated how corporations can influence society for the better.

Final Thoughts: Enabling the World

The life story of Francoise Bettencourt Meyers is a compelling example of how one person's influence may have a long-lasting effect on the globe.

Her narrative is one of personal strength, tenacity, and steadfast commitment to improving the lives of others.

Francoise epitomizes the spirit of a strong woman who used her position for the greater good, from inheriting a renowned family history to emerging as a pioneering corporate leader and philanthropist.

Throughout her life, Francoise imparted wisdom and served as an inspiration to future generations:

1. *Francoise's leadership style* was purpose-driven and dedicated to having a positive social effect. She served as an example of how business and charity may combine, illuminating how corporations can affect societal change for the better.

2. *Perseverance in Adversity:* Francoise demonstrated the value of keeping calm and dignity in the face of difficulties by handling problems and disagreements with elegance. Her tenacity served as a reminder that obstacles must be overcome to leave a lasting legacy.

3. *Women's Empowerment:* By breaking down obstacles and paving the way for other women to seek leadership positions in a traditionally male-dominated field, Francoise empowered women. She is an inspiration to women all around the world because of her commitment to gender equality and women's empowerment.

4. *Social Responsibility:* Francoise's dedication to charitable work and humanitarian issues brought attention to how money may spur progress. She made use of her money to fund programs that intended to improve the globe and boost local communities.

The legacy of Francoise Bettencourt Meyers is one of kindness, inventiveness, and hope for the future.

Her effect will be felt well beyond the beauty industry and the boundaries of her family's enterprises, as she considers the legacy she will leave behind for future generations.

Her long-lasting legacy will be one of supporting women's rights, encouraging sustainability and social responsibility, and empowering people and communities.

Her vision for the future is a society where money is utilized to bring about good change, corporations lead with a purpose, and women are given the freedom to assume leadership positions.

Francoise aims to encourage people to accept their responsibilities to have a good effect on society via her family's charitable endeavors and the continuous success of L'Oreal.

We take the inspiration and lessons from Francoise Bettencourt Meyers' life journey with us as we say goodbye to this compelling biography of an independent heiress.

Her narrative will continue to serve as a source of inspiration, showing us that each person can effect change and leave a lasting legacy that will inspire future generations.

Made in the USA
Las Vegas, NV
05 January 2024

83926349R00026